Color and Create
Vintage War posters

*20 Poster designs to help
release your creative side*

Connect with us online to
- Share your colorings with other coloring enthusiasts
- Get free downloads of some of our designs
- Find out about our up-and-coming books
- Get discounts and enter competitions

Our Facebook Page:
www.facebook.com/colorandcreate

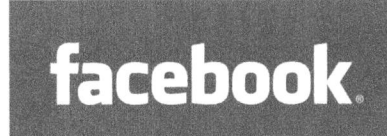

Our Facebook group:
www.facebook.com/groups/colorandcreate

On Twitter:
www.twitter.com/CCColoringBooks

On Pinterest:
www.pinterest.com/colorandcreate

Color Test Page

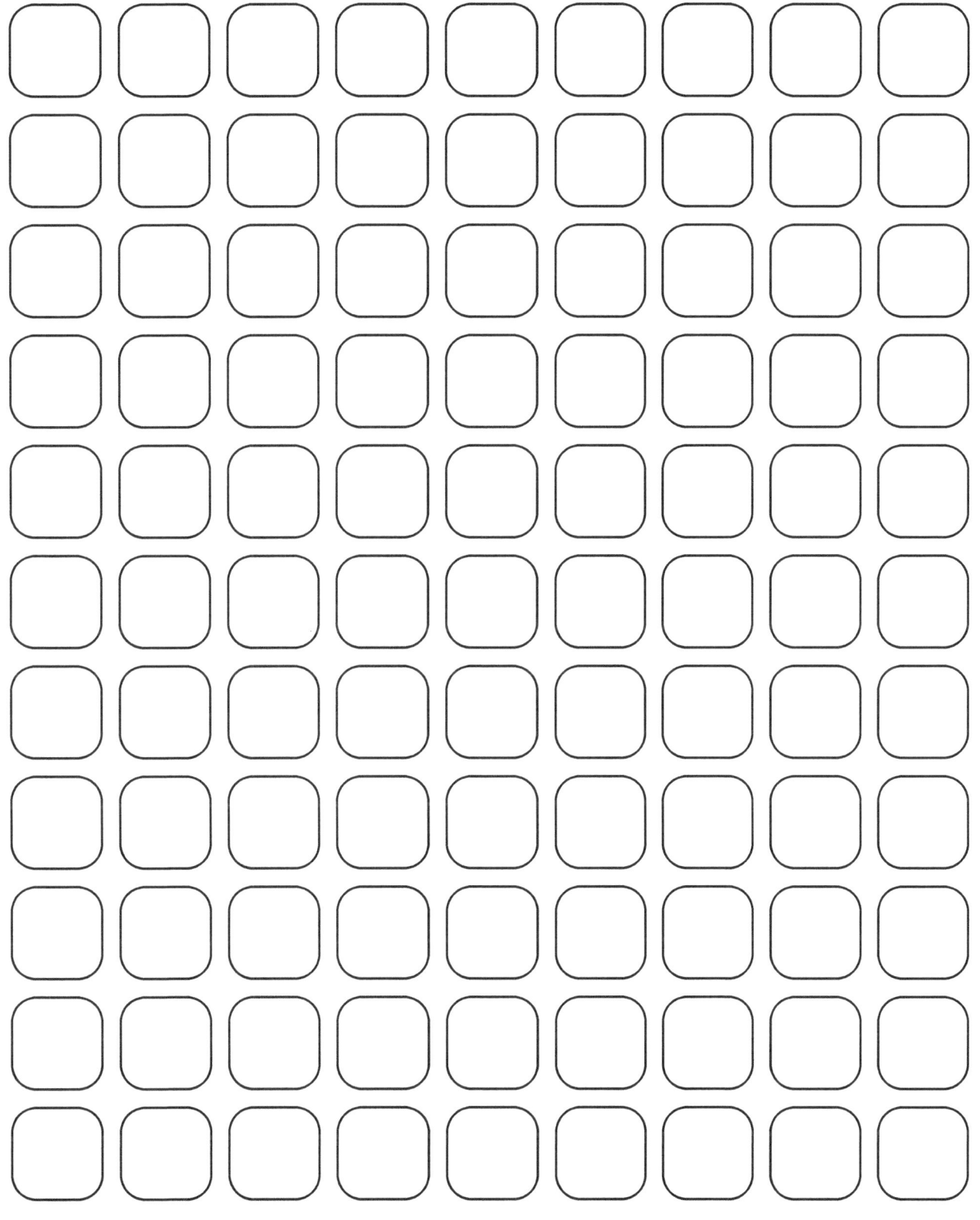

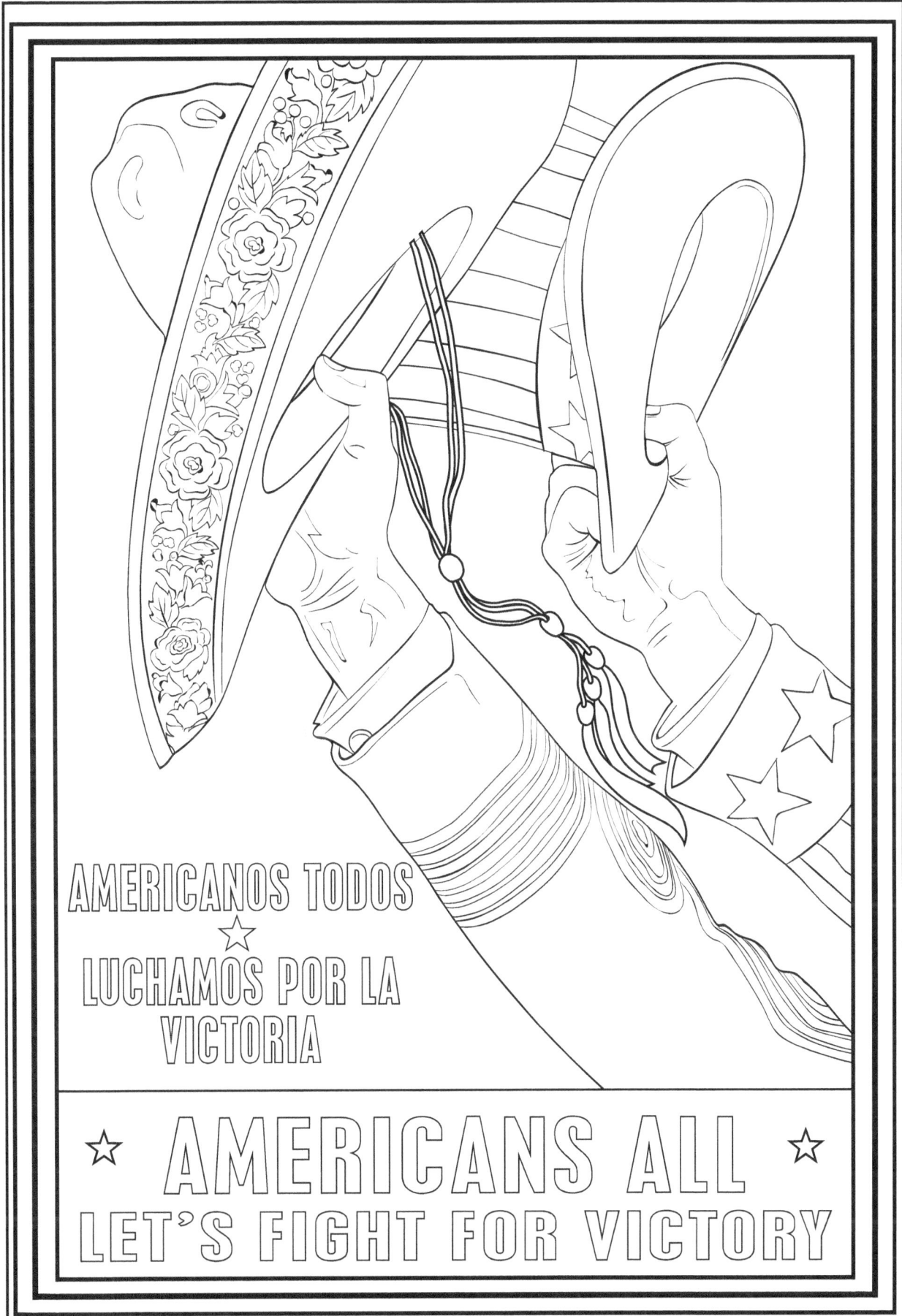

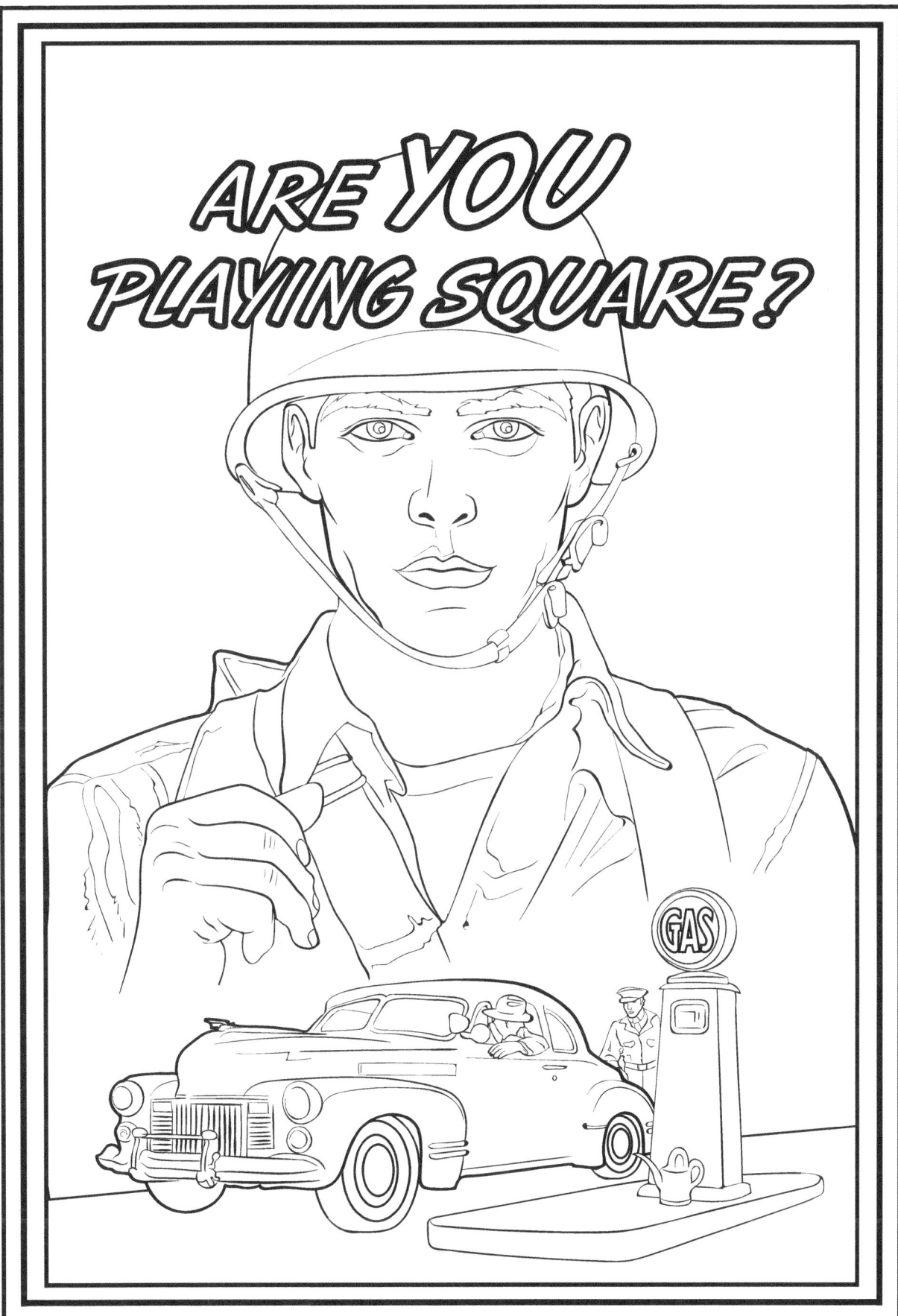

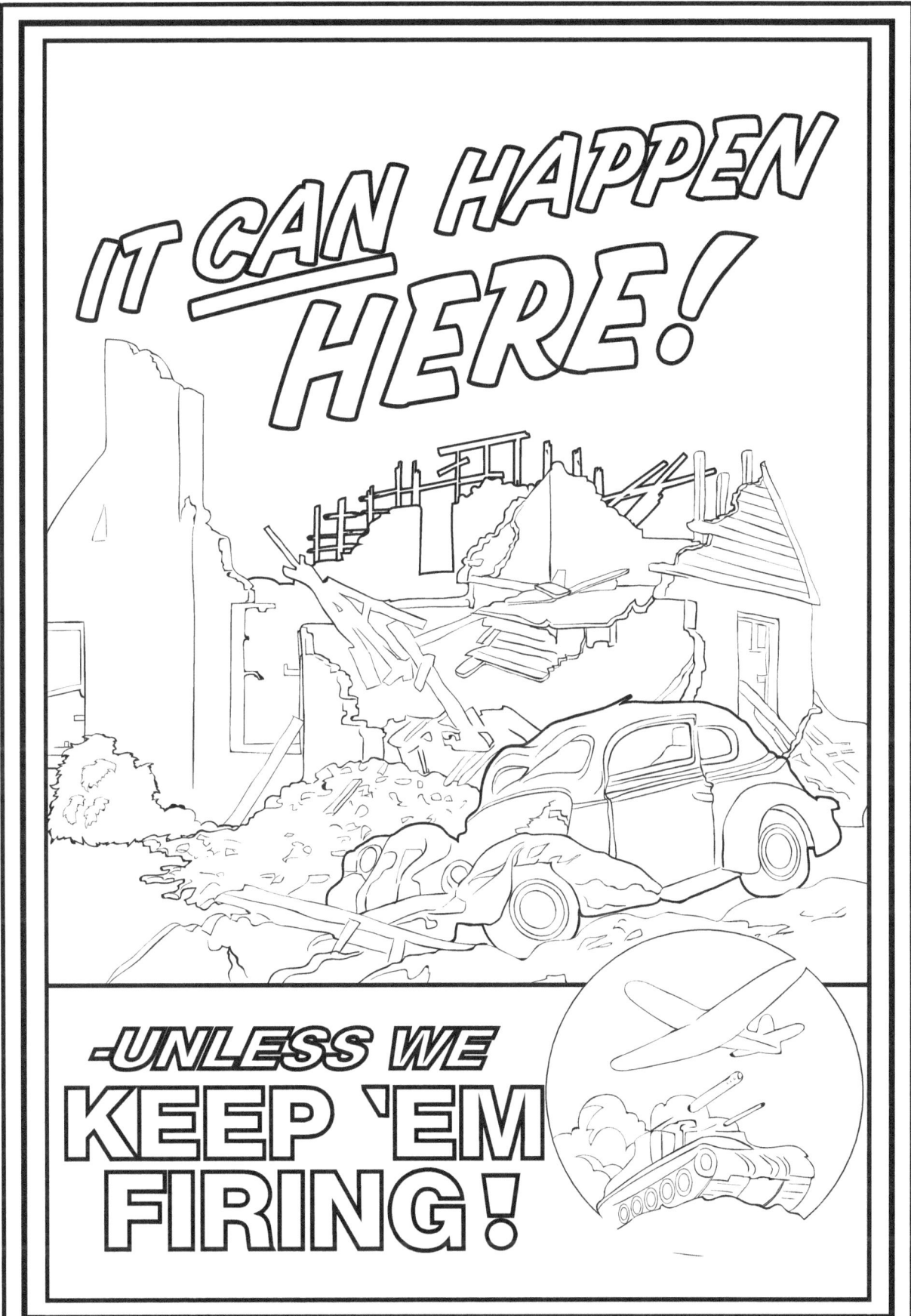

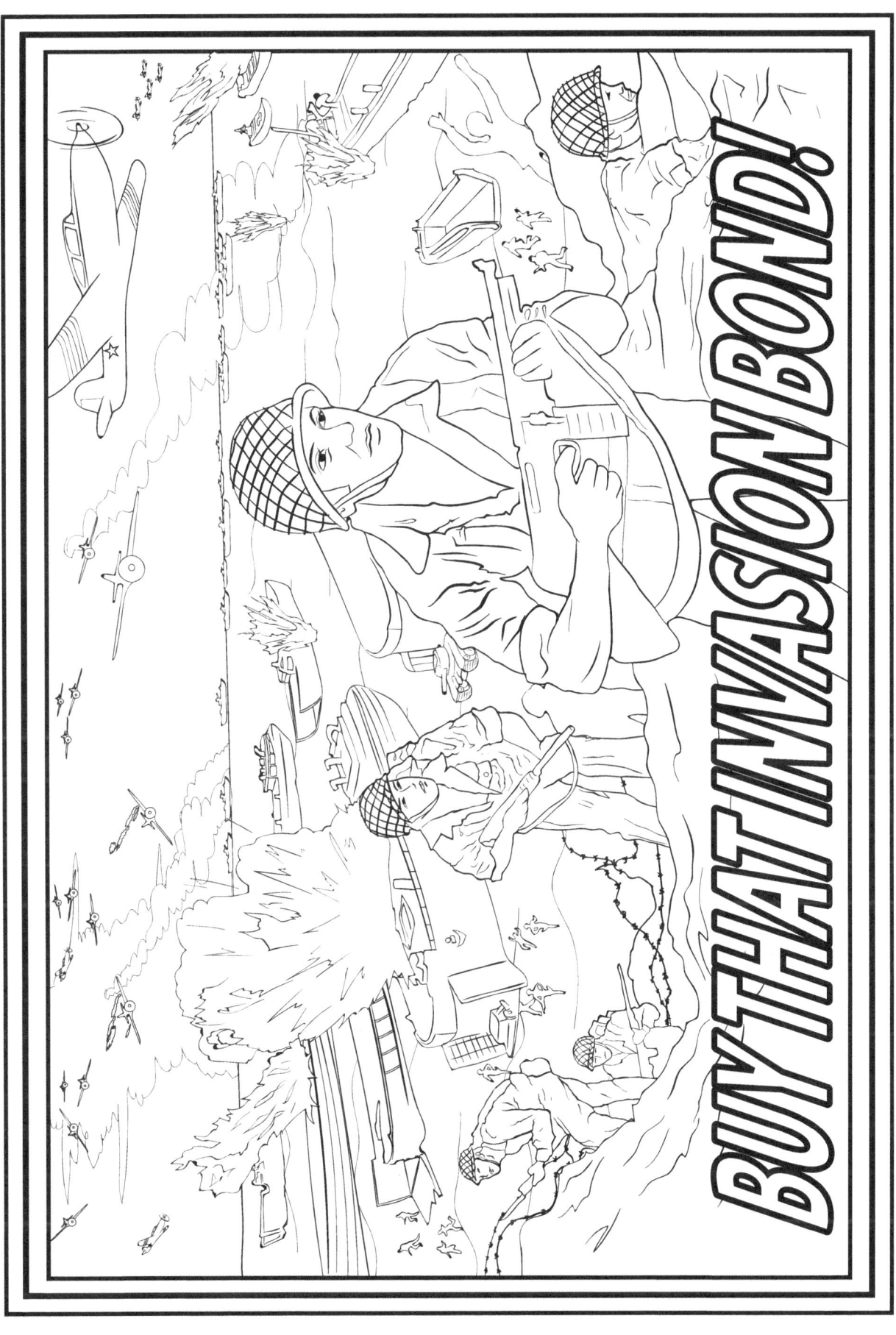

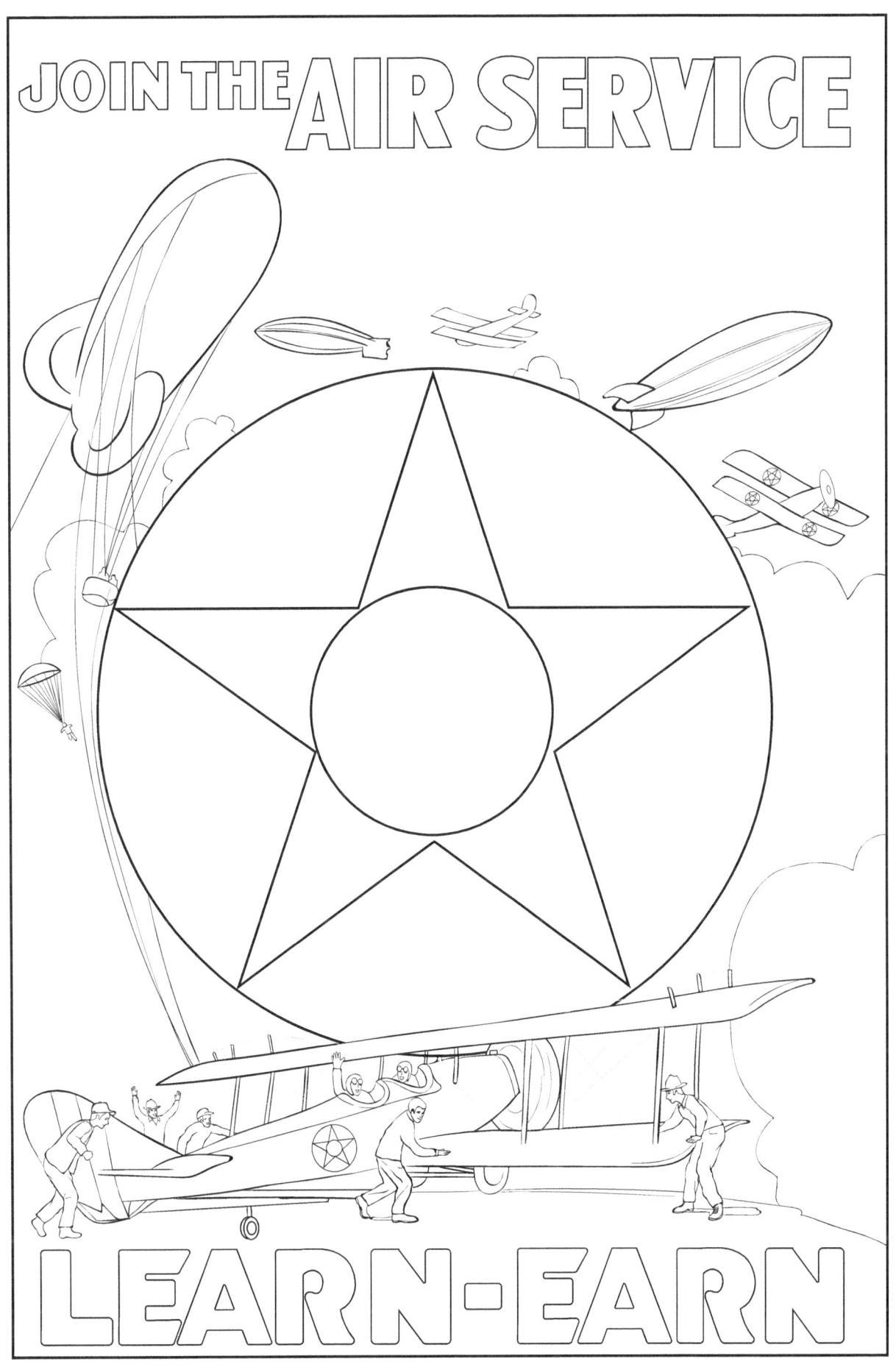

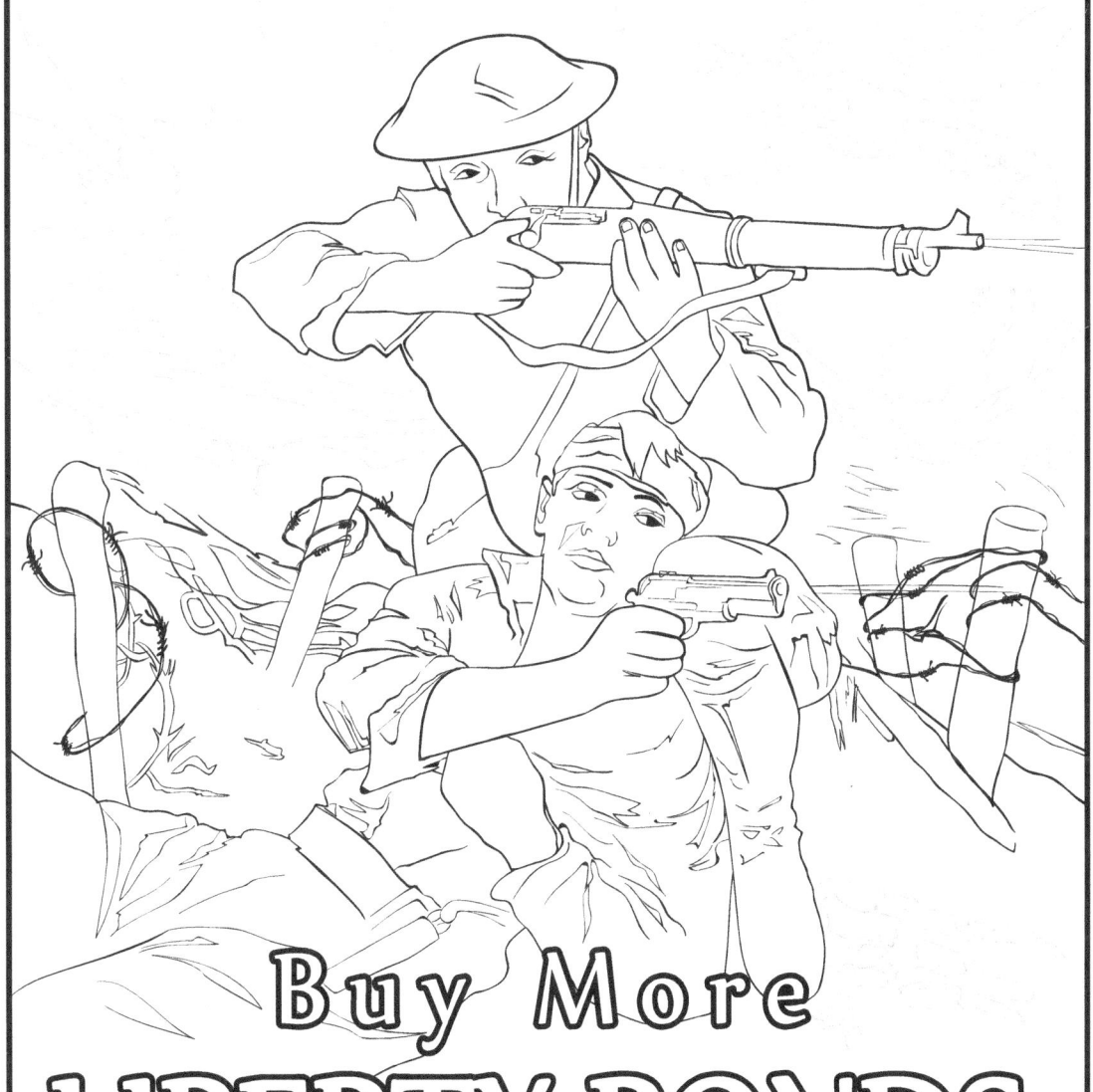

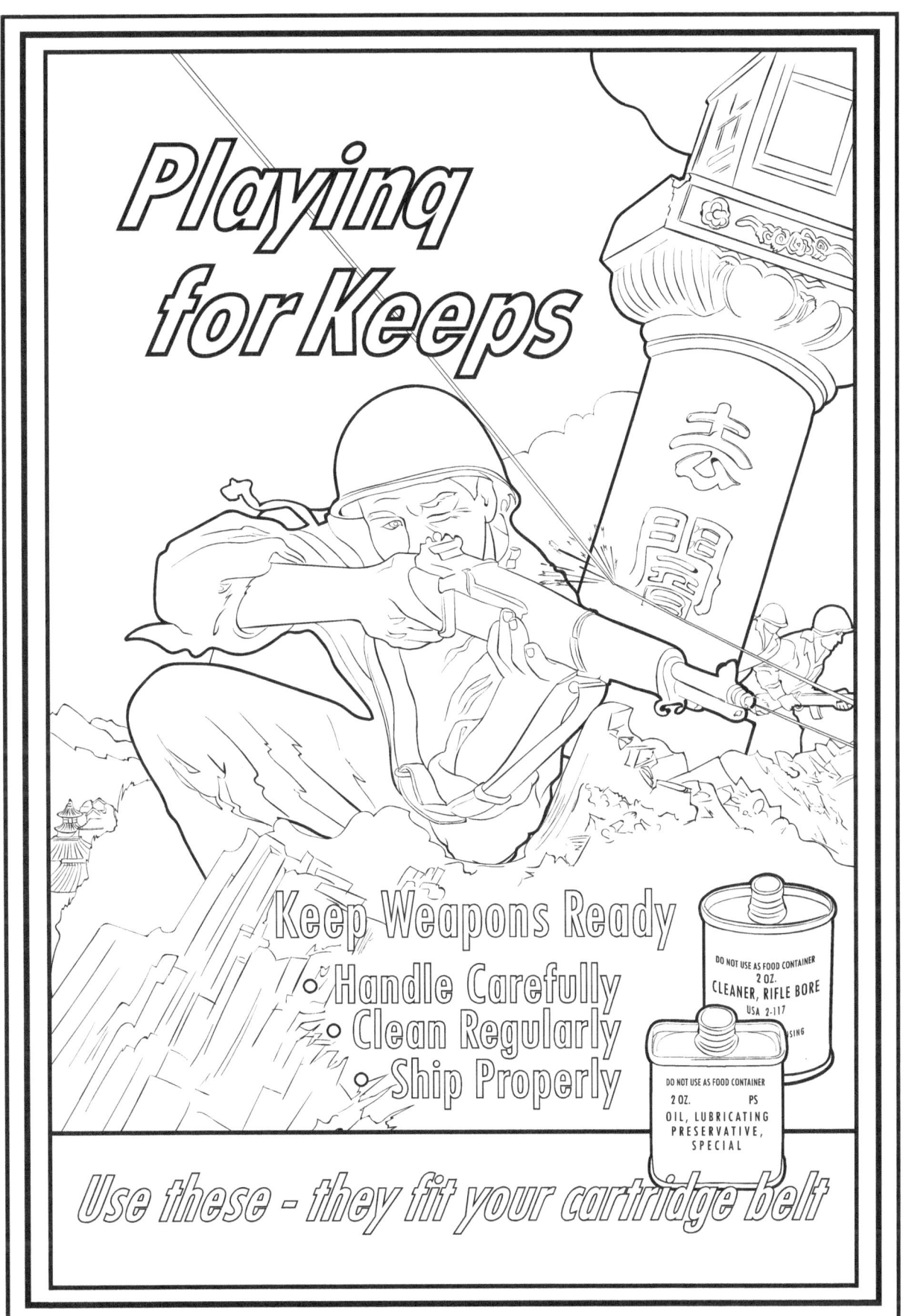

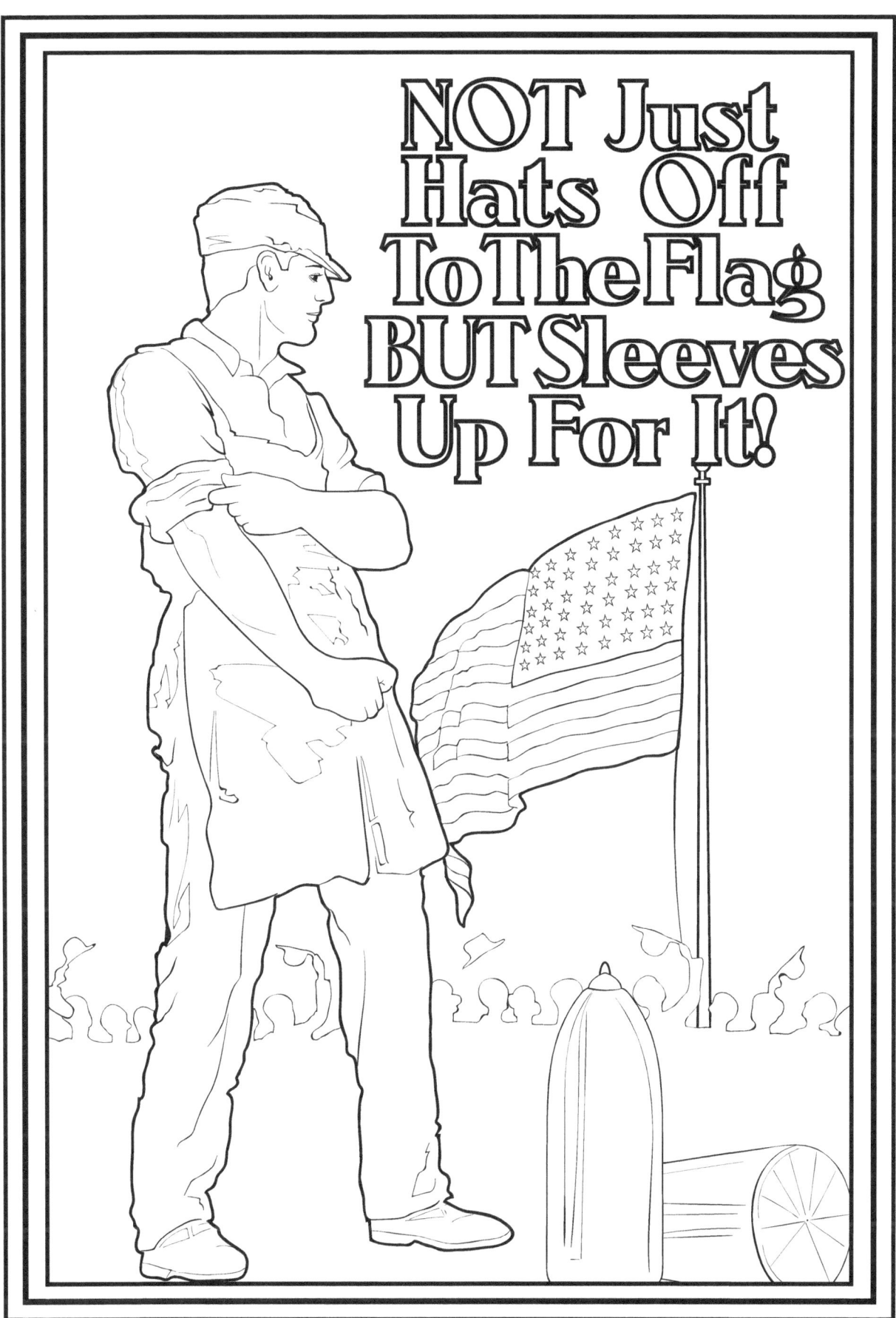

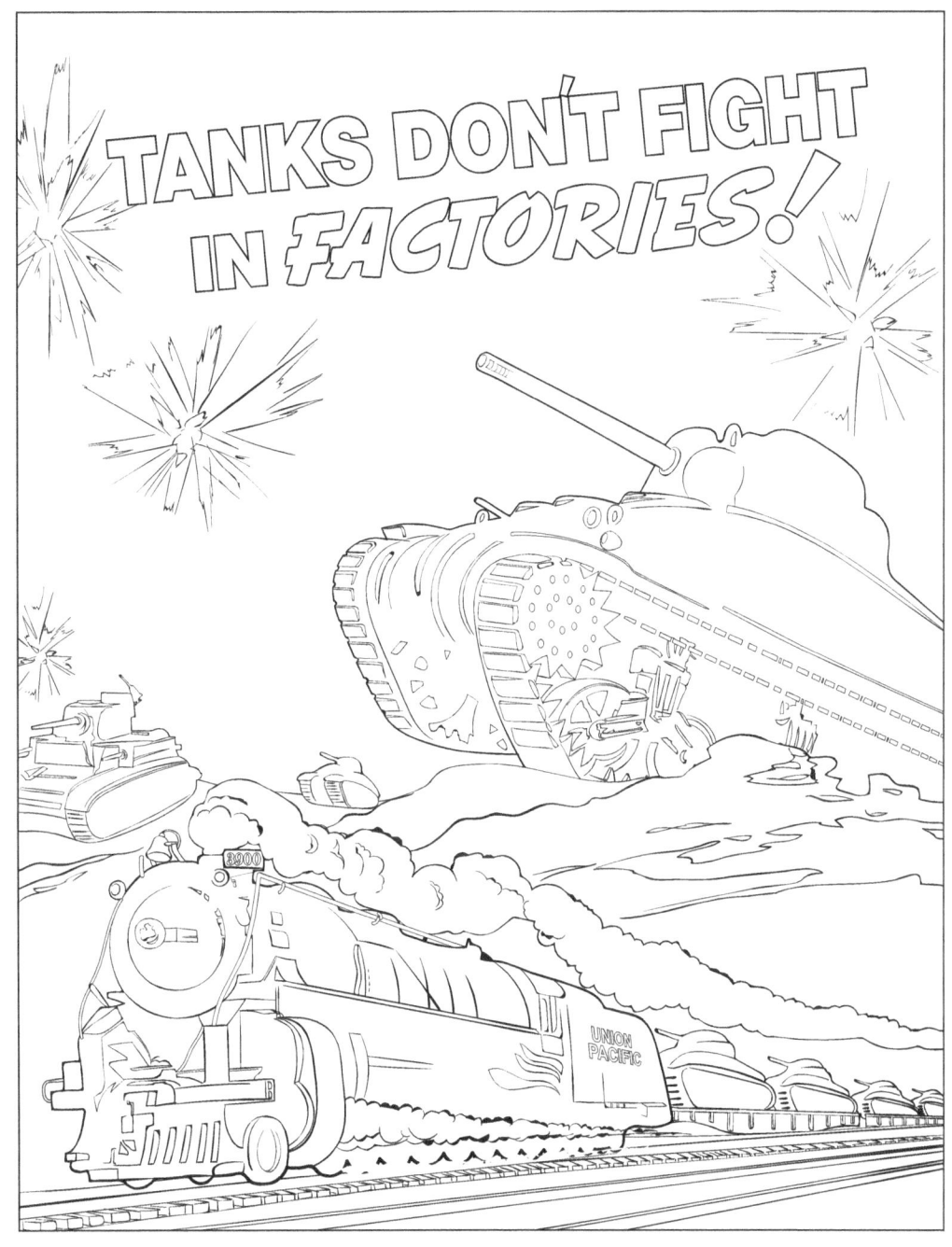

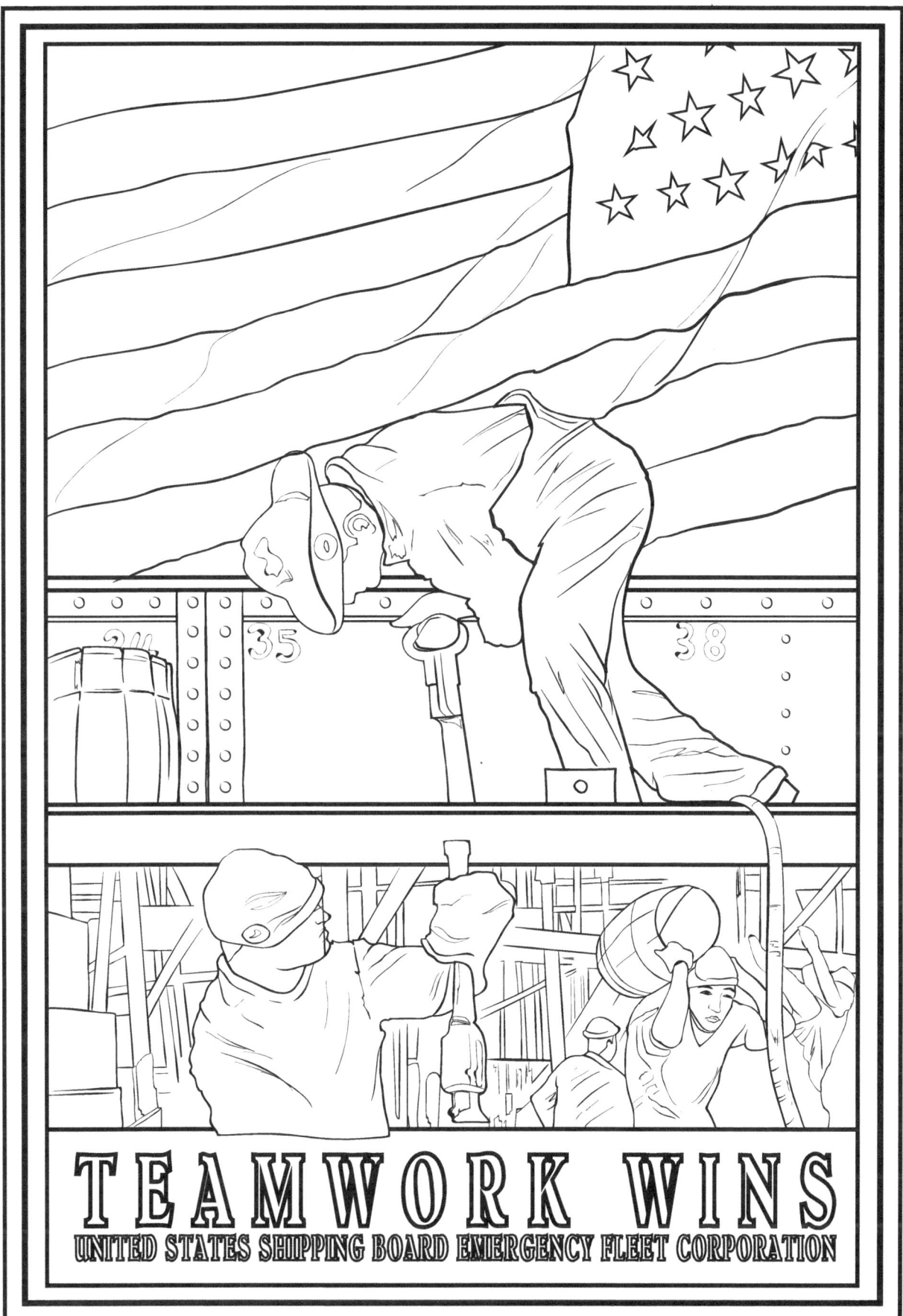

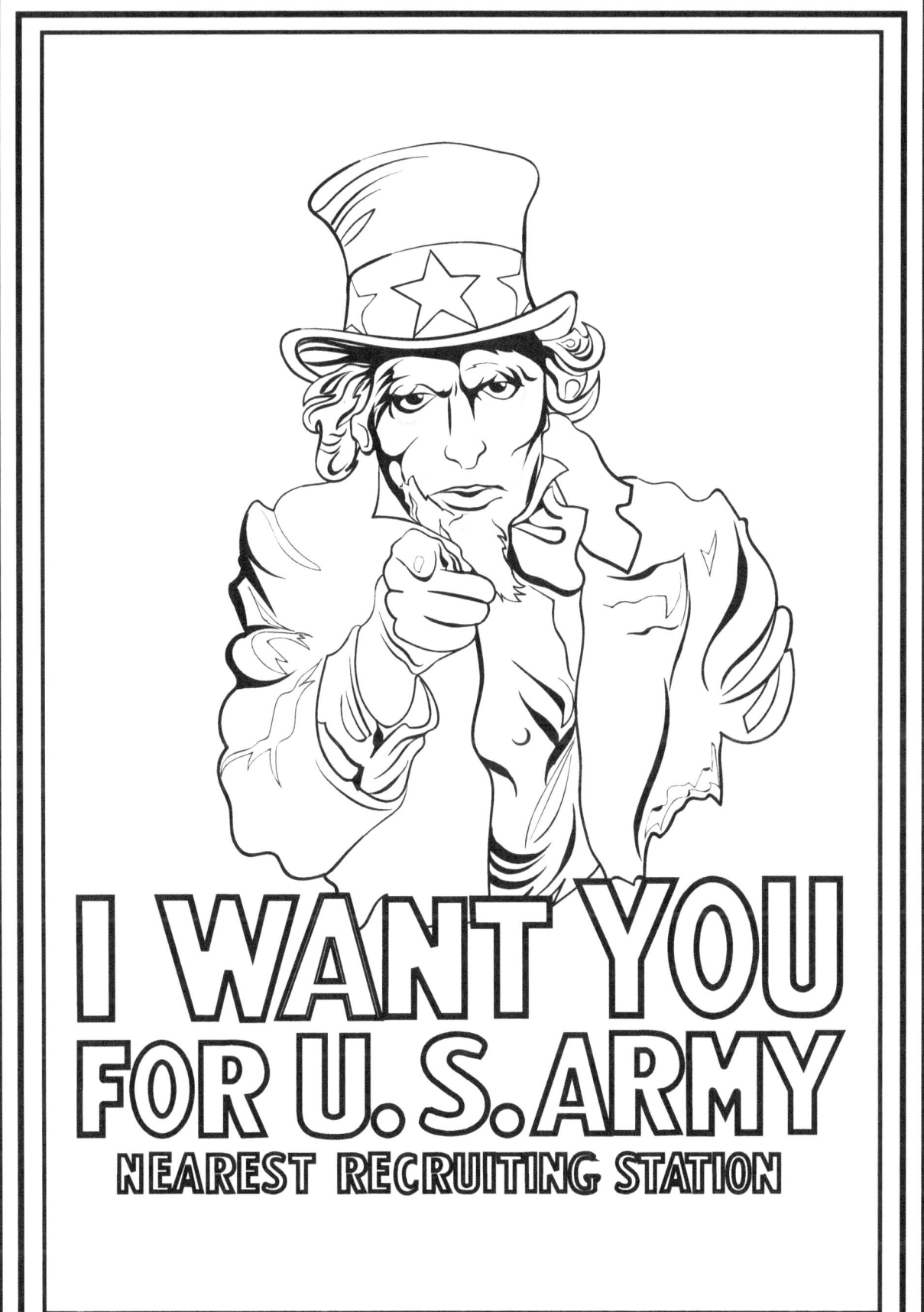

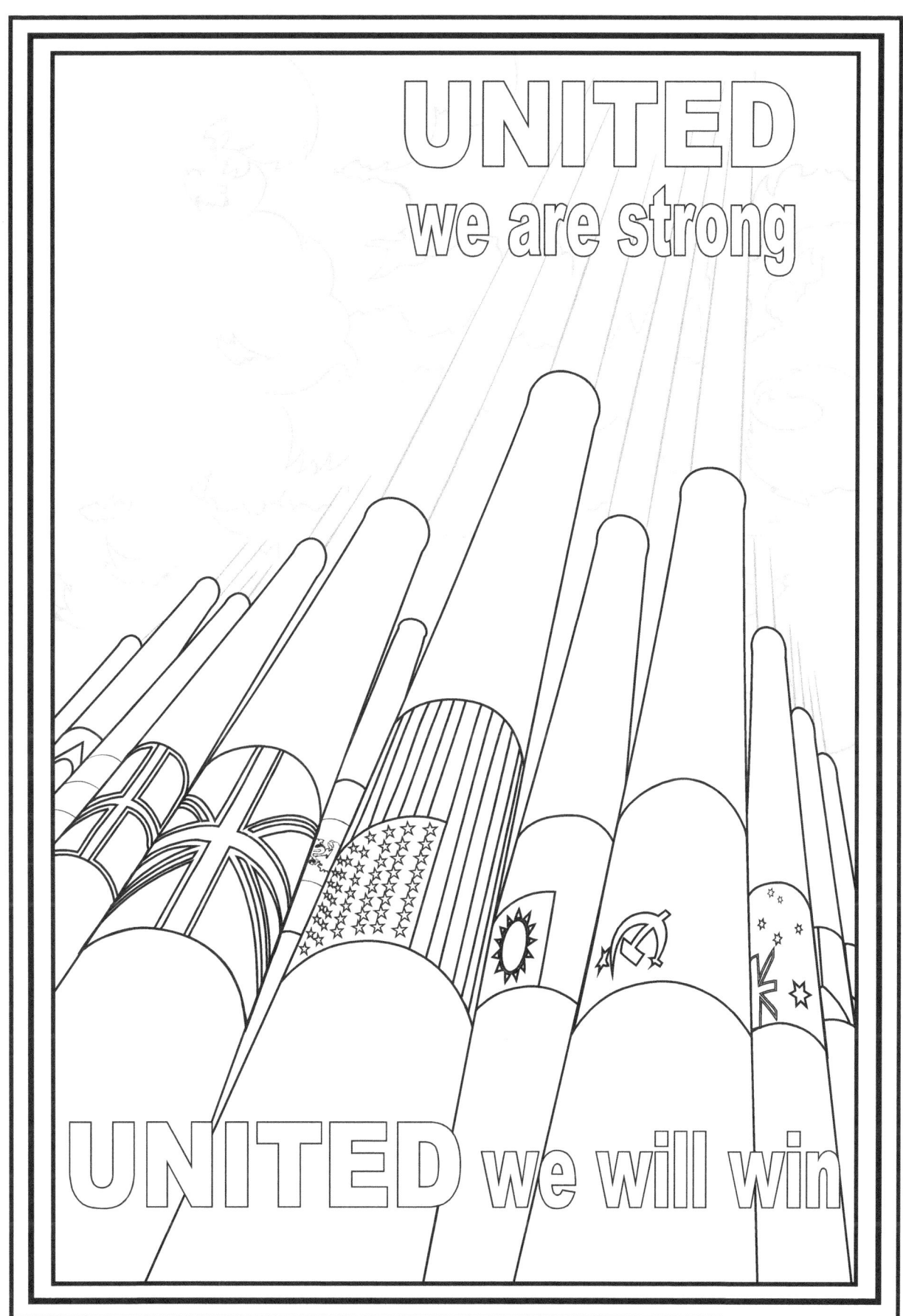

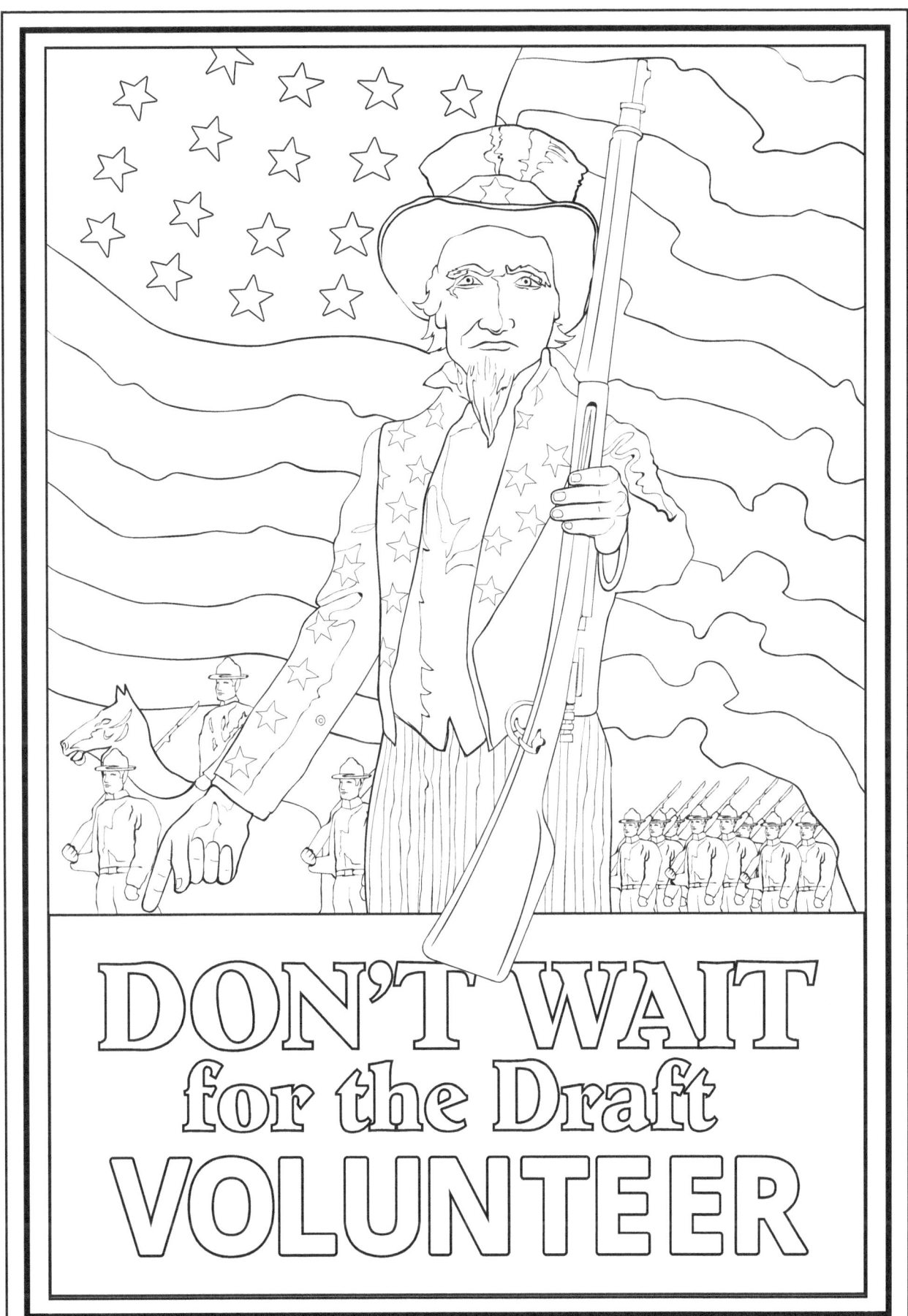

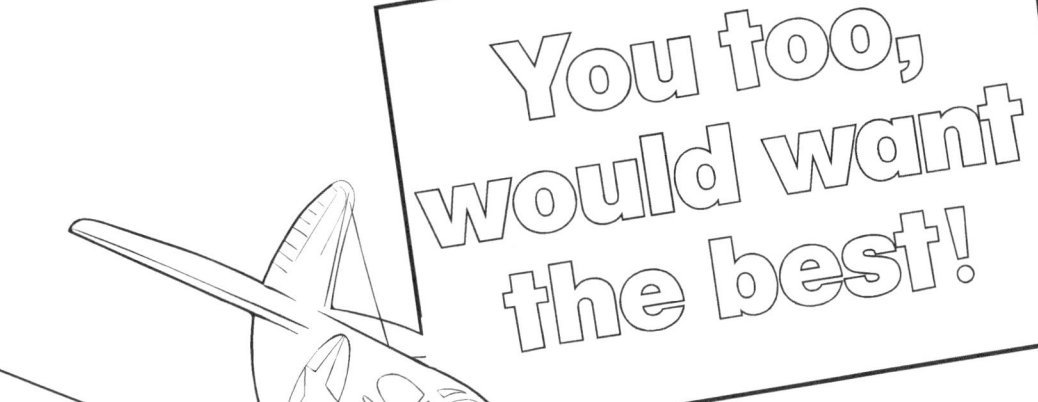

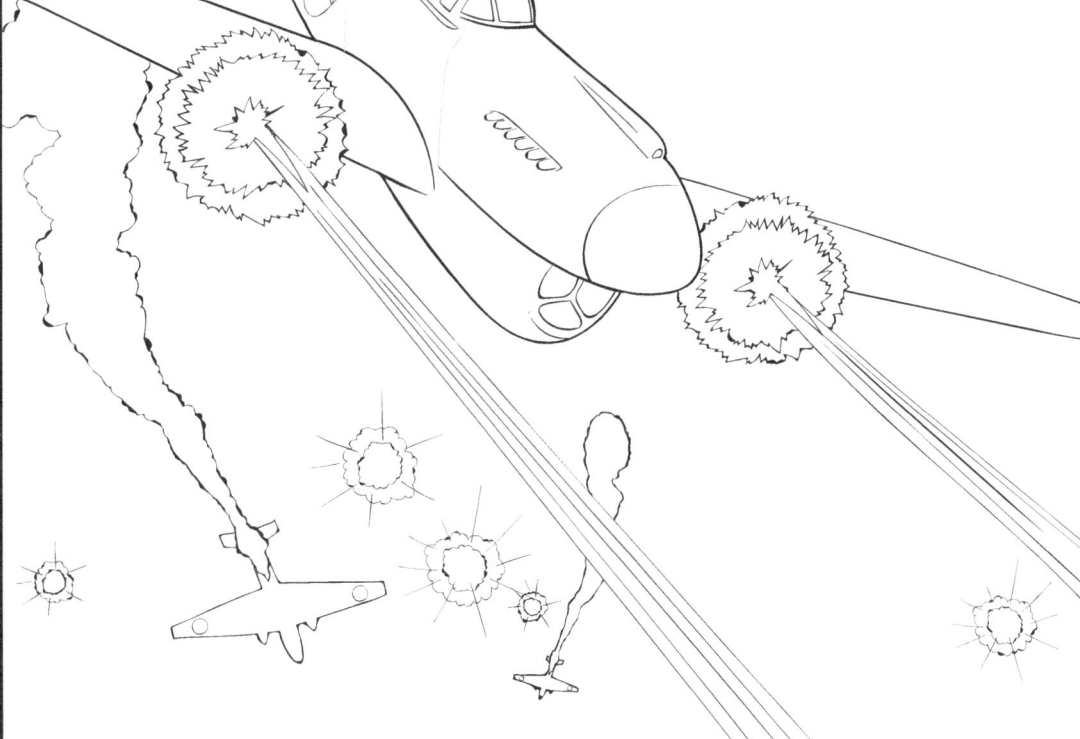

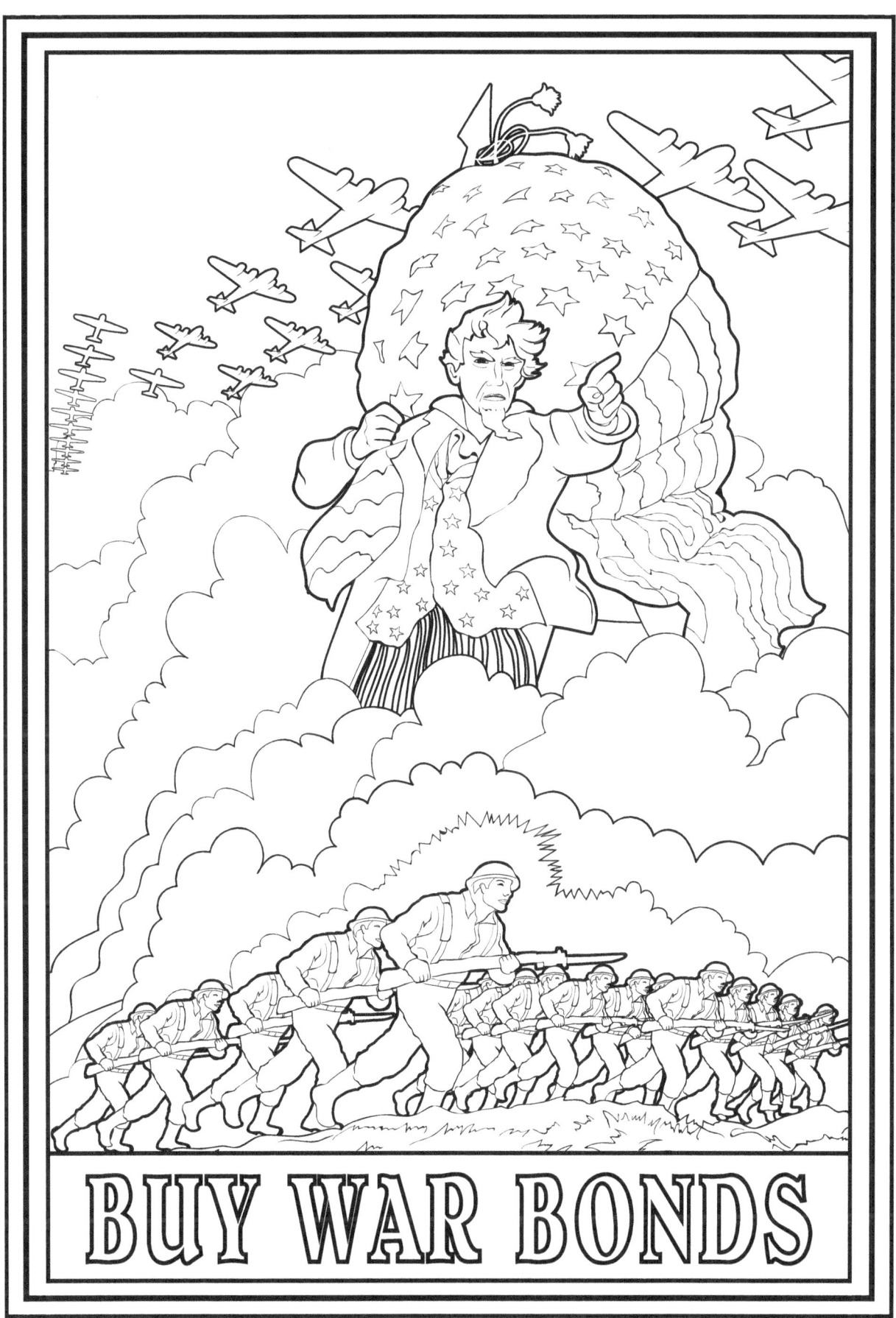

BUY WAR BONDS

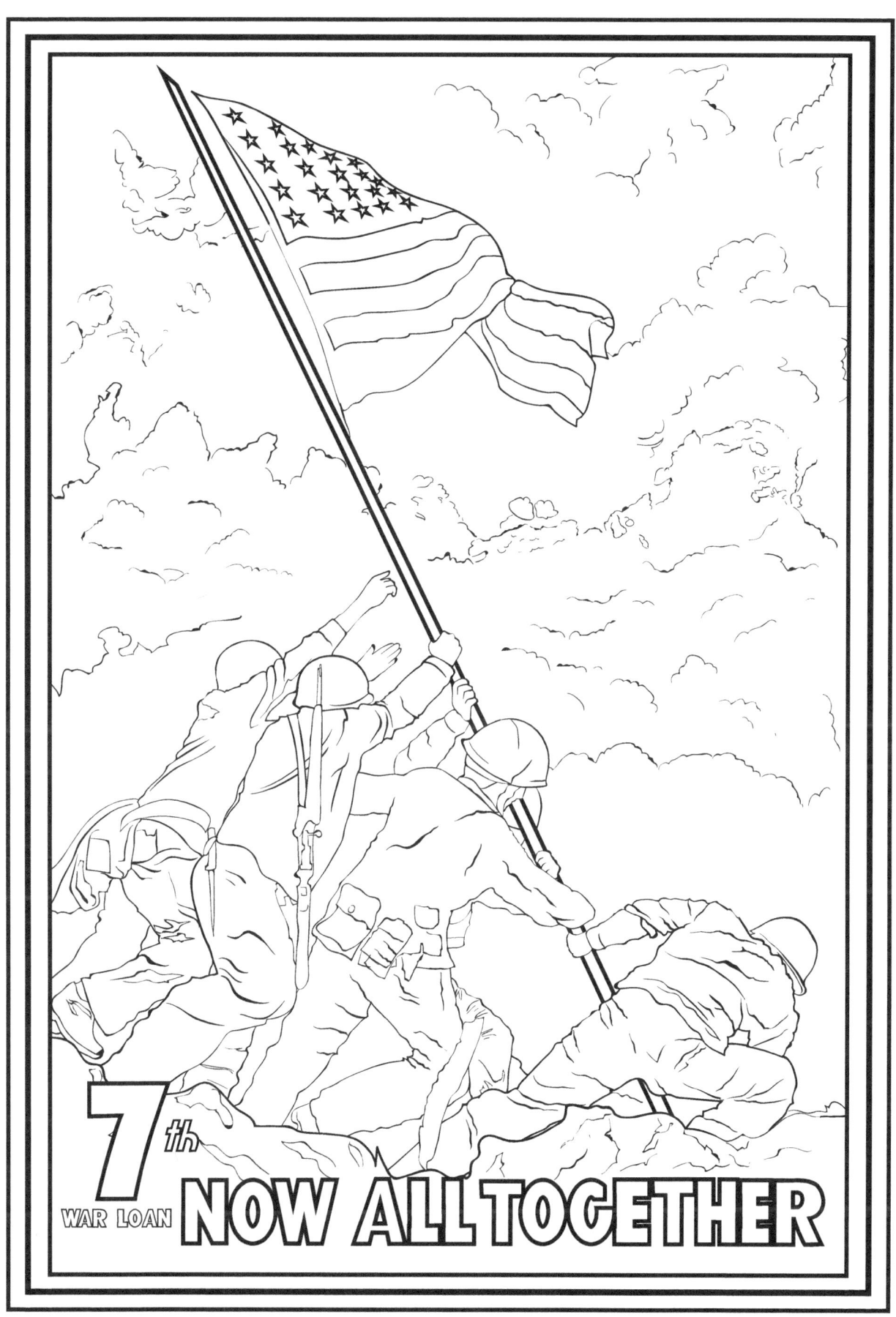

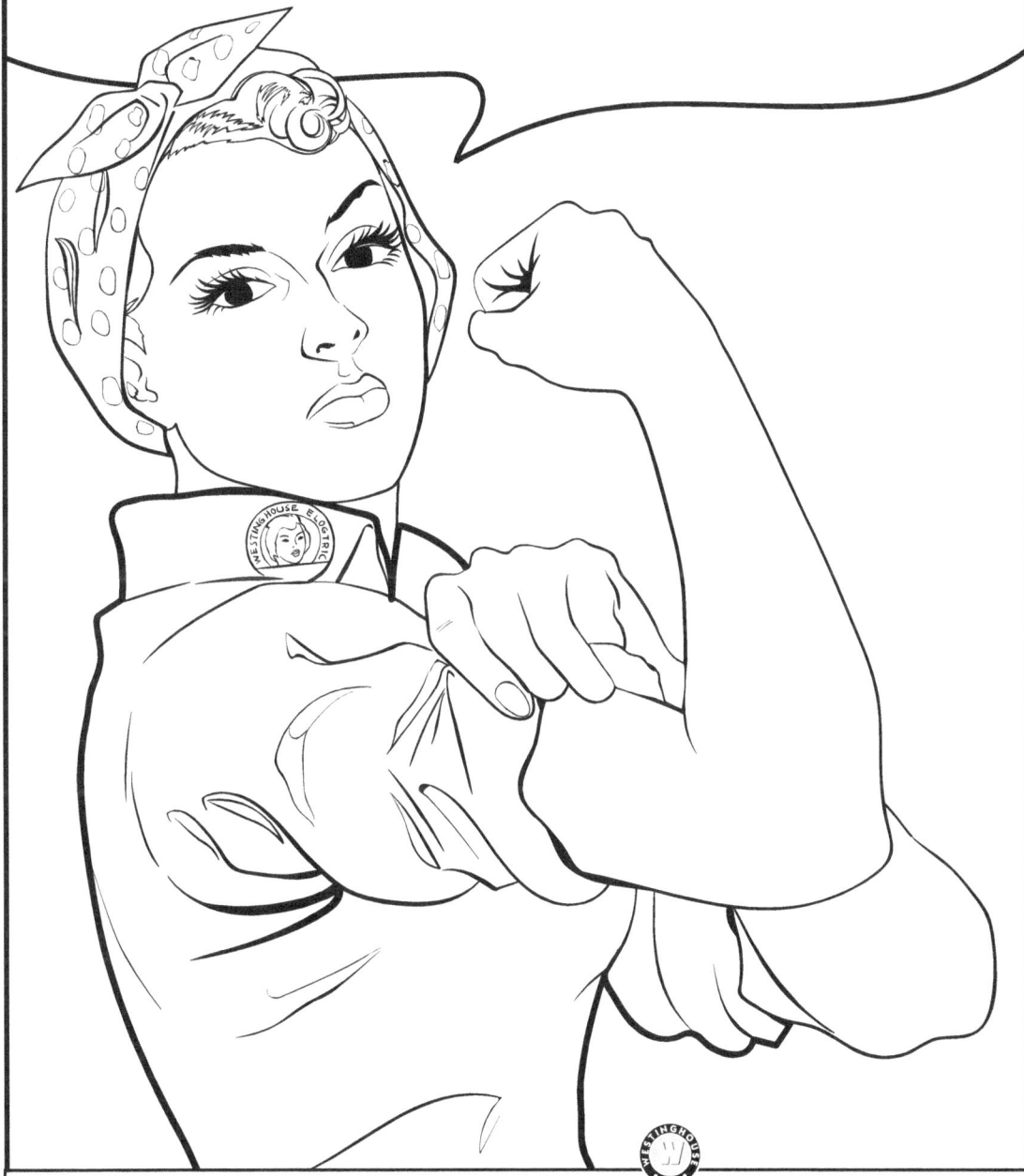

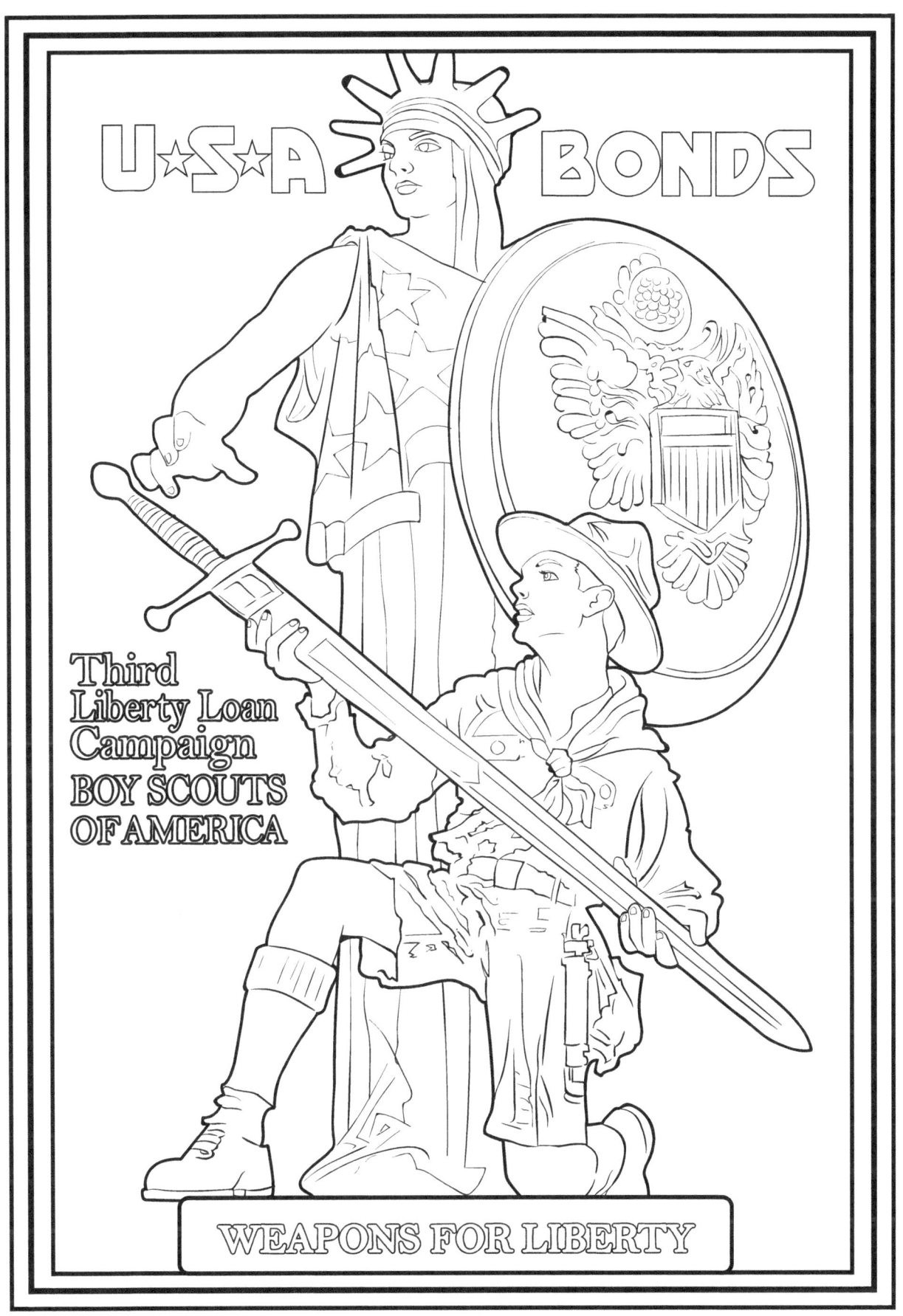

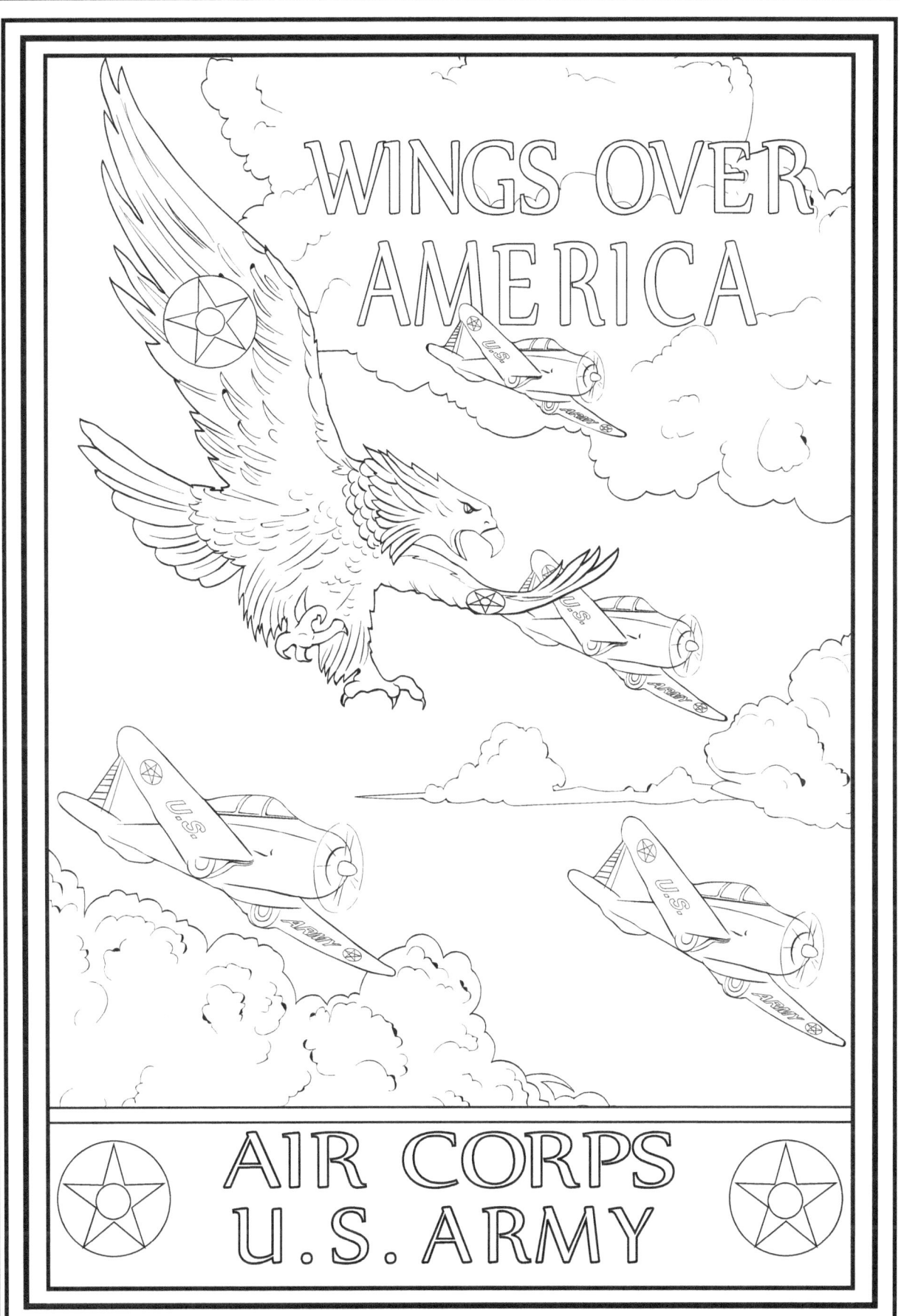

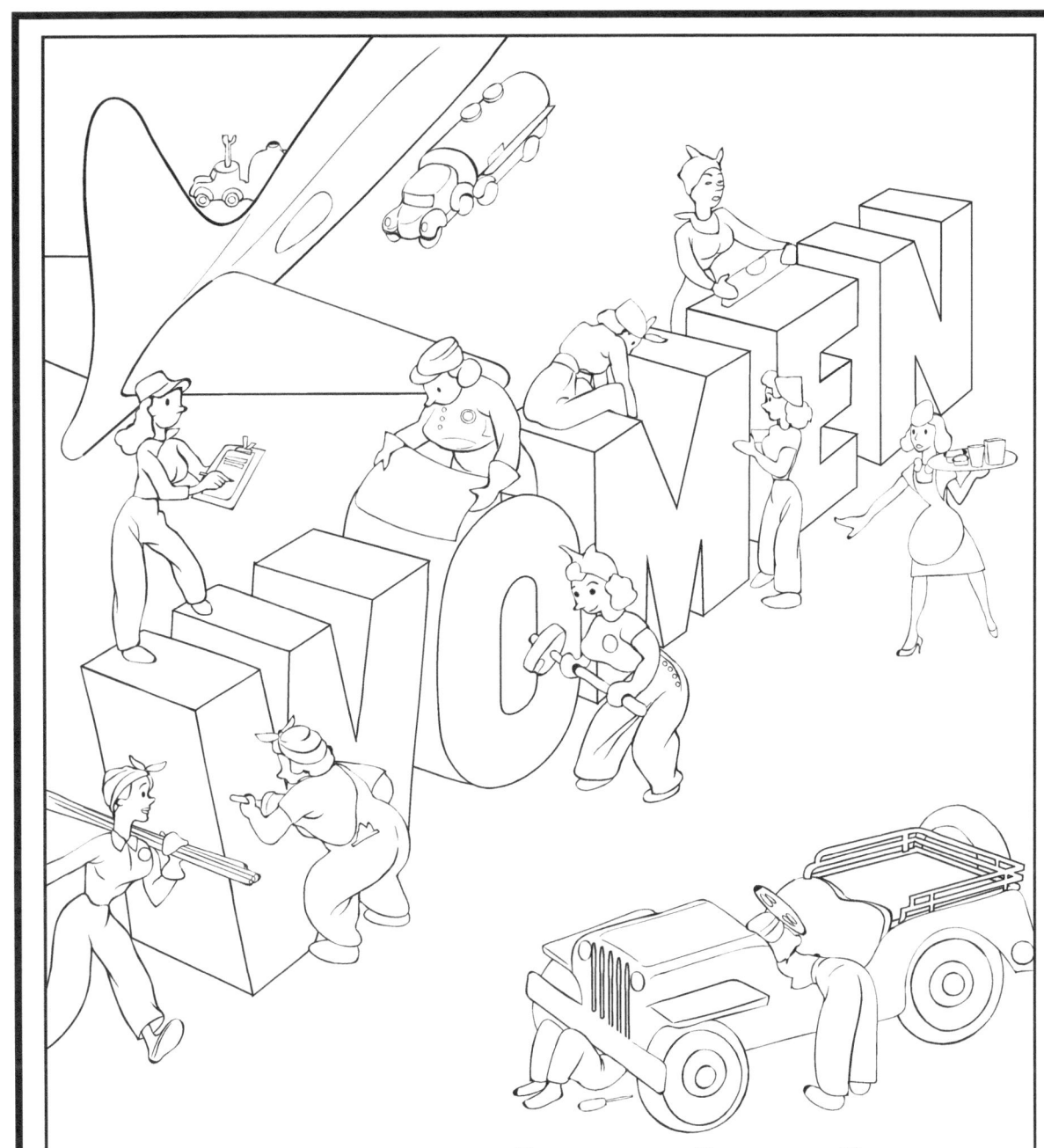

www.ingramcontent.com/pod-product-compliance
Lightning Source LLC
Chambersburg PA
CBHW080139240526
45468CB00009BA/2538

9 7 8 1 9 4 4 1 1 9 2 2 5